PIZZA AND PASTA

CLAUDIA MARTIN

Enslow Publishing
101 W. 23rd Street
Suite 240
New York, NY 10011
USA

enslow.com

Published in 2019 by Enslow Publishing, LLC.
101 W. 23rd Street, Suite 240, New York, NY 10011

Editors: Sarah Eason and Jennifer Sanderson
Designers: Paul Myerscough and Simon Borrough
Picture Researcher: Claudia Martin

Cataloging-in-Publication Data
Names: Martin, Claudia.
Title: Pizza and pasta / Claudia Martin.
Description: New York : Enslow Publishing, 2019. | Series: Cooking skills | Includes glossary and index.
Identifiers: ISBN 9781978506671 (pbk.) | ISBN 9781978506404 (library bound) | ISBN 9781978506343 (ebook)
Subjects: LCSH: Pizza—Juvenile literature. | Cooking (Pasta)—Juvenile literature. | Cookbooks—Juvenile literature
Classification: LCC TX770.P58 M35 2019 | DDC 641.82'48—dc23

Printed in the United States of America

To Our Readers: We have done our best to make sure all website addresses in this book were active and appropriate when we went to press. However, the author and the publisher have no control over and assume no liability for the material available on those websites or on any websites they may link to. Any comments or suggestions can be sent by e-mail to customerservice@enslow.com.

Photo Credits: Cover: Shutterstock: AngleStudio: bc; stockcreations: tc; tanja-vashchuk: br; Uber Images: bl. Inside: Shutterstock: 275847: pp.24–25; Africa Studio: p.15b; Anna Prytkova: p.18; Antonio Danna: p.44; AS Food Studio: pp.36–37, 38–39; asife: p.39r; casanisa: pp.1t, 5t; Cesarz: pp.30–31; Cultura Motion: p.15t; Da-ga: pp.22–23; Dmytro Mykhailov: p.23c; dotshock: pp.16–17, 46; DronG: pp.18–19; Ekaterina Kondratova: pp.20–21; elenamych: p.13c; Elena Shashkina: p.31l; Elena Talberg: p.38; Farbled: p.33c; Gamzova Olga: p.32; GCapture: p.45; George Rudy: pp.10–11; Goskova Tatiana: p.23t; HBRH: p.30; Helena Zolotuhina: p.21t; hiphoto: pp.14–15; Kazlouski Siarhei: pp.42–43; Kostiantyn Ablazov: p.39l; Iakov Filimonov: p.31r; Irina Goleva: pp.26–27; Jiri Hera: p.34r; Joe Gough: p.21c; Joshua Resnick: p.35; JumlongCh: pp.1b, 9; lenetstan: pp.13b, 28–29, 37t, 40–41; Lindsay Stone: p.37b; MagicBones: p.43r; margouillat photo: p.21b; Monkey Business Images: pp.6–7, 27b; Monzino: p.34l; nenetus: pp.34–35; Ngukiaw: pp.8–9; Nick Lundgren: p.33t; oneinchpunch: p.13t; Osadchaya Olga: p.22b; Owl_photographer: pp.22t, 46–47, 48; Petrut Romeo Paul: p.11; Pressmaster: pp.4–5; Radu Bercan: pp.2–3, 16r; Rawpixel.com: pp.5b, 43l; saschanti17: p.42; Schab: p.25; Shebeko: pp.44–45; Snowbelle: p.27t; stockcreations: pp.12–13; StockphotoVideo: pp.29, 32–33; Svitlana Pimenov: p.24; Tom Gowanlock: p.41; Vgstockstudio: p.19; Wararit Prasitsat: p.16l; William Perugini: p.33b.

CONTENTS

CHAPTER 1
GET COOKING!

Want to cook up a meal for your friends? Pizza and pasta are great places to start as they are easy to make, and delicious!

Italian Cooking

Pasta and pizza are part of Italian cuisine. So why are these foods some of the most popular in kitchens across the United States—and around the globe? The answer is that the classic combinations of tomatoes, garlic, cheese, and herbs always taste great and are not too difficult to put together, even for a beginner. In addition, pizza and pasta are really filling, so you will feel sufficiently satisfied after eating.

Good for You

This brings us to an important question: are pasta and pizza healthy? There are many benefits to the Mediterranean diet. For example, tomatoes and the other vegetables in Italian recipes are full of fiber and nutrients. Olive oil is an excellent oil as it is low in saturated fat, the "bad" fat that can lead to heart disease.

Not so Good

What is not so healthy is eating too many refined grains, like those found in white pasta and most store-bought pizza crusts. These are high in calories and low in fiber and nutrients. Try buying—or making—pasta and pizza dough from whole grain flour.

Dietary Requirements

If you are cooking for vegetarian friends, all the recipes in this book can be made meat- and fish-free. Take a look at the "Switch It Up" boxes at the start of each chapter for ideas. Before planning a meal for friends, find out if they have any other special dietary needs, such as a wheat or gluten intolerance or allergy. Pastas and pizza doughs made from other grains, as well as some roots and legumes, are available in many grocery stores. They may be labeled "gluten-free."

Store It Up

As you flip through the recipes in this book, you will see that some ingredients come up again and again. If you would like to cook a lot of Italian food, keeping these staple ingredients in your pantry or refrigerator will mean you can always rustle up a tasty meal in minutes. Begin with these basics:

- Pasta of your choice
- Ready-made pizza crusts
- Olive oil
- Canned tomatoes
- Parmesan cheese
- Eggs
- Fresh basil

READ THE RECIPE

So where do you start? The first thing to do is choose a recipe that you think your friends will enjoy.

Where to Start

If you want to serve pasta, choose between the three ways that Italian chefs cook pasta: tossed in a sauce (see Chapters 2, 3, and 4), baked in the oven (see Chapter 5), or floating in a soup (see Chapter 6). If you want to serve your pasta in a sauce, the recipes in Chapters 2, 3, and 4 offer saucy classics that are traditionally cooked with three of the most popular pasta shapes: spaghetti, tagliatelle, and fusilli (also called rotini). If you would like to cook some pizza, turn to Chapter 7.

Be Prepared

Once you have chosen a recipe, check out the ingredients and equipment you will need. Each of the recipes serves four people, so multiply up or divide down as needed. Make a list of any missing ingredients, then head to the store. Remember that some ingredients will keep for a long time (like dried pasta and canned tomatoes) while others need to be bought only a day or two before cooking (like fresh herbs and meat).

Timing Is Everything

Always overestimate how long it will take to cook a recipe, so you are not rushed by hungry diners while you are still preheating the oven. Read the recipe instructions carefully, before putting knife to garlic. To help make sure you do not miss any ingredients, they are listed in the order they are used. If you are not sure you have all the necessary cooking skills, look at the "Mastering the Basics" sections at the start of each chapter.

How Much, How Hot?

In these recipes, measurements are given in ounces (oz), followed by grams (g), as well as cups, followed by milliliters (ml) or liters (l). There are 240 ml in each cup. Sometimes, you will be told to add a teaspoon (tsp) or tablespoon (tbsp) of an ingredient. There are 5 ml in each teaspoon and 15 ml in each tablespoon. When a "handful" or a "pinch" is suggested, the exact quantity is less important—add more or less for a stronger or weaker taste.

Oven temperatures are given in degrees Fahrenheit (°F), followed by degrees Celsius (°C). If you are not sure how hot to have the stove, start low then adjust upward—it is better to cook slowly than to burn!

...OR GO YOUR OWN WAY

The recipes in this book are only guidelines to get you started on your cooking journey.

Taste and See

The first time you cook a recipe, it is easiest to follow the instructions closely. When you sit down with friends to enjoy the results, consider what you like about the flavors and textures and what you do not. Is there too much sauce or not enough? Do you dislike the taste of anchovies? Could your plate benefit from an extra punch of flavor from some chili flakes, another clove of garlic, or some fresh basil?

Cook Like a Chef

The "Chef's Tip" boxes alongside each recipe will help you because they suggest ways of adding different, richer, or spicier flavors. The "Switch It Up" boxes on the first page of each chapter will give you many more ideas for switching ingredients. However, do not be bound by these suggestions—let your own taste buds be your guide. Chefs always trust their instincts!

Try Something Different

In the pasta recipes that follow, a particular sort of pasta is recommended for each dish, usually because it is the traditional pasta to use. However, traditions are meant to be changed! There are many other pasta shapes you could switch into these recipes—in fact, there are around 310 different pasta shapes made in Italy, although many of those may not be available in your local store.

Keep It Clean

Hygiene is very important in any kitchen. Before you cook:

- Wash your hands thoroughly.
- Make sure all your work surfaces and equipment are clean.
- If you have long hair, tie it back.
- Wash all produce under cold running water.
- When working with raw meat or fish, wash your hands after handling, and use a different cutting board and knife from the one for other ingredients.
- Never serve undercooked meat or fish—make sure there is no pink meat and that fish is cooked all the way through.
- Check the use-by dates on all ingredients.
- Do not leave food out of the refrigerator for more than two hours.

CHAPTER 2
SPAGHETTI

Everyone knows what spaghetti looks like—it is the classic pasta shape of long, rounded strands. Spaghetti soaks up sauce and flavor, making it slippery but delicious to eat.

Kinds of Spaghetti

Although it may look similar on your plate, there are different sorts of spaghetti. One of the most popular is dried durum wheat semolina spaghetti (*pasta secca di semola*), made from wheat flour and water.

Most grocery-store spaghettis are made from refined flour, which has had the germ (kernel) and bran (outer layer) of the grain removed. A healthier option is whole wheat spaghetti, which looks browner and contains more fiber and nutrients.

Another type of spaghetti is made from egg pasta (*all' uovo*), in which egg has been added to the flour and water. Egg pasta can be bought dried or fresh, from the chilled section. If you cook with fresh pasta, remember to reduce the boiling time.

Mastering the Basics
Al Dente Spaghetti

Italians eat their pasta *al dente*, which means "to the tooth." In other words, pasta should be firm to the bite—springy and slightly chewy. Here is how to make perfect al dente spaghetti (or any other type of pasta):

1. In a large pot, pour in enough water to submerge the pasta.
2. Add 1 tbsp salt. This adds flavor and raises the boiling temperature of the water so your pasta will cook really well.

3. Bring the water to a boil—you need to see a lot of big, rolling bubbles.
4. Add the spaghetti to the water. After one minute, stir to ensure the pasta is submerged and not sticking together or to the pan. Stir every few minutes.

Switch It Up

Once you know how to cook spaghetti, you do not always need to follow a recipe. Just mix up some ingredients that taste good together. How about frying some anchovies, chili flakes, and garlic in olive oil then stirring through cooked spaghetti? Or try frying mushrooms and garlic in olive oil and sprinkling with Parmesan and parsley? How about frying some bacon with those mushrooms?

5. Follow the cooking time on the package, but two minutes before the pasta should be ready, use a slotted spoon to take out one strand. Let it cool before tasting. If it is too chewy, give it another minute and check again.
6. To drain pasta safely, put a colander in an empty sink, then pour the contents of your pot into it.

SPAGHETTI BOLOGNESE

This is a great quick-and-easy meal for days when you need filling food fast.

You Will Need

1 tbsp olive oil
1 medium onion, peeled and chopped
1 garlic clove, peeled and sliced
17 oz (500 g) ground beef
15 oz (425 g) can of tomato soup
14 oz (400 g) spaghetti
2 oz (55 g) Parmesan cheese, grated
Sprig of basil to garnish

Instructions

1 Heat the olive oil in a large, thick-bottomed pan, then fry the onion and garlic over a low heat until the onion is softened.
2 Add the ground beef. Stirring regularly, cook until it is browned (so no pink meat can be seen).
3 Pour in the tomato soup, then cook on a medium heat for ten minutes, until the sauce has thickened.
4 While the meat sauce is simmering, cook the spaghetti (see page 11 for help) in another large saucepan. Follow the instructions on the package.
5 Drain the spaghetti, split it between four bowls, then dish out the meat sauce.
6 Sprinkle with the Parmesan and garnish with basil leaves.

Pasta on the run—job done!

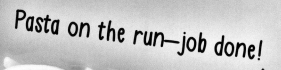

CHEF'S TIP

Once the meat sauce has cooled to room temperature, you can store it in the freezer for when you need a really super-speedy meal.

13

SPAGHETTI ALLA PUTTANESCA

This spicy favorite is quick to make—and will be wolfed down even quicker.

You Will Need

1 tbsp olive oil
2 garlic cloves, sliced thinly
15 oz (425 g) can of chopped tomatoes
1 tbsp capers
2 anchovies, chopped
1 handful of black olives
1 bunch of basil
1 pinch dried chili flakes
Salt and pepper
14 oz (400 g) dried spaghetti

Instructions

1 Heat the oil in a large frying pan, then gently fry the garlic for two minutes.
2 Add the tomatoes, capers, anchovies, olives, chili, and a few basil leaves. Simmer for ten minutes, then season to taste.
3 In the meantime, follow the instructions on the package to cook the spaghetti.
4 Drain the spaghetti, mix in the sauce, and garnish with sprigs of basil.

Super-speedy pasta!

CHEF'S TIP

For a quick and easy "kick,"
add a few drops of Tabasco
to your sauce.

basil

CHAPTER 3

TAGLIATELLE

Tagliatelle is a long, ribbon-shaped pasta often served with a meat sauce, but you can serve it however you like.

Making Ribbons

The name "tagliatelle" comes from the Italian word *tagliare*, which means "to cut." Tagliatelle is usually made from egg pasta (see page 10), rolled thin and cut into strips around 0.2 inches (5 mm) wide. Fettuccine ("little ribbons") is wider and thicker, around 0.25 inches (6.5 mm) wide. Wider still is pappardelle (from *pappare*, which means "to gobble up").

Extra Sauce

The addition of egg to the pasta makes it easier to shape, but today some factory-produced tagliatelle is made without egg. The rougher texture of egg pasta means it soaks up extra sauce, making your recipes even more flavorful. Tagliatelle and other ribbon-shaped pastas can be bought dried or fresh.

Switch It Up

To make a tasty and protein-full vegetarian dish using tagliatelle, follow the carbonara recipe on page 18 but switch the bacon for 10 oz (285 g) of mushrooms. You will need to fry them for longer than the bacon, for around six minutes. For a richer taste, mix porcini mushrooms in with less expensive varieties, such as button mushrooms. Porcini mushrooms are often sold dried, so rehydrate them in hot water for around twenty minutes before using them.

Mastering the Basics
Preparing Garlic

Garlic is featured a lot in Italian food, giving sauces a rich taste and mouth-watering aroma. A useful skill is knowing how to quickly peel and slice or crush a clove of garlic:

1 Take a bulb of garlic, which contains several sections called cloves. Pull a clove from the bulb.
2 Lay the clove on a cutting board. Place the blade of a wide knife flat on top of the clove. Using the heel of your hand (keeping your skin and fingers well away from the blade), press down the knife to crack the clove's papery skin, then peel it away.
3 Slice off the hard root end of the clove.
4 To slice the clove, use a fine, sharp knife to cut away five to seven thin sections. Start with the point of the knife on the board and use a gentle rocking motion. Keep your fingers out of the way!
5 To crush the clove, put the skinned clove in a garlic press if you have one. If not, slice it crossways, then lengthways, and then mash it with a fork.

TAGLIATELLE ALLA CARBONARA

Once you have the hang of carbonara, you will never want to stop making this tasty, rich sauce.

It is the heat from your pasta that cooks the eggs.

You Will Need

14 oz (400 g) dried tagliatelle
3 large eggs
$1/3$ cup (80 ml) heavy cream
3 oz (85 g) Parmesan cheese, grated
1 tbsp olive oil
7 oz (200 g) bacon, chopped
2 garlic cloves, peeled and crushed
Salt and pepper

Instructions

1 Bring a large pot of water to a boil. Add the tagliatelle and cook for ten minutes or follow the package instructions.
2 While your pasta is simmering, beat together the eggs, cream, and 2 oz (55 g) of the Parmesan in a mixing bowl.
3 Heat the oil in a large pan. Fry the bacon for two to three minutes until it is lightly browned, then add the garlic. Fry for one minute.
4 Drain the pasta. Remove the pan of bacon from the heat, then pour in the hot pasta and the egg mixture. Stir until the pasta is coated in creamy sauce.
5 Sprinkle with the remaining Parmesan cheese and season to taste.

CHEF'S TIP

If your sauce is too thick, add 1 tbsp of the water from your simmering pasta pot.

TAGLIATELLE WITH SMOKED SALMON

The contrast between the smoked salmon and tangy lemon makes this recipe such a favorite.

You Will Need

14 oz (400 g) dried tagliatelle
2 tbsp butter
3 garlic cloves, peeled and thinly sliced
1 cup (240 ml) crème fraîche
4 tbsp Parmesan cheese, grated
Juice of 1 lemon
14 oz (400 g) smoked salmon, cut into strips
Salt and pepper
Dill to garnish

Instructions

1 Put the tagliatelle into a pot of boiling water.
2 While the pasta is simmering, melt the butter in a large frying pan. Add the garlic and cook over a very low heat for five minutes.
3 Stir in the crème fraîche and Parmesan cheese with the garlic.
4 When the pasta is cooked, drain it, and stir it into the pan with the sauce. Add the lemon juice and smoked salmon. Season to taste. Mix well, then serve, garnished with a little dill.

Dill has a fresh, grassy flavor.

21

CHEF'S TIP

If you cannot find crème fraîche in your local grocery store, heavy cream will work just as well.

CHAPTER 4
FUSILLI

Fusilli, or rotini, are corkscrew-shaped pasta. Sauces become stuck inside the folds and creases of the pasta, making it burst with taste.

Types of Fusilli

Fusilli were developed in southern Italy by wrapping fresh pasta strips around a rod, or spindle (*fuso*), then letting them dry. Today, fusilli can be bought dried and fresh, made from whole or processed wheat, and in a variety of colors, such as red (made using beetroot), green (using spinach), and black (using cuttlefish ink). Fusilli and other corkscrew pastas can be paired with any kind of sauce and served hot or cold.

What's in a Name?

Here is a useful tip when you are buying pasta or trying to impress your friends: when a pasta name ends "ini," it is usually a smaller version of the shape. When a pasta name ends "oni," it's a bigger version. So tiny twists are fusillini, while bigger twists are fusilloni.

Mastering the Basics
Perfect Pesto

Made with pine nuts, basil, and Parmesan cheese, pesto is a classic sauce that can be mixed into fusilli or any other pasta to pep it up. You can buy ready-made pesto sauce from the market. Just keep the jar refrigerated once it is opened. You can also make your own pesto if you have a food processor. Follow these steps to make 1 cup (240 ml) of sauce:

pesto

1 Use about 5 oz (140 g) fresh basil. Pick the leaves from the stems and wash thoroughly.
2 Put the leaves in a food processor along with 3 oz (85 g) pine nuts, 3 oz (85 g) grated Parmesan cheese, 1 peeled and chopped garlic clove, and a little salt. Turn on the processor for a few pulses.
3 Add 3 tbsp water and 6 tbsp olive oil. Process for ten or twenty seconds, until you have a grainy sauce.
4 Your pesto will keep in the refrigerator for up to a week.

Switch It Up

Fusilli are often used in pasta salads as they hold a pesto sauce, mayonnaise, or vinaigrette so well. If you are looking for more salad ideas, try a classic Caprese by mixing fusilli with sliced ripe tomatoes, mozzarella cheese, fresh basil, and a wine vinegar and olive oil vinaigrette. Another option is to use the same vinaigrette but swap in salami and some sundried tomatoes.

PESTO PASTA SALAD

Serve this simple-to-make salad as a main meal for four or as a side dish for six to eight people.

Grab a fork, this is delicious!

You Will Need
14 oz (400 g) fusilli
1 cup (240 ml) pesto (to make your own, see the recipe on page 23)
10 oz (285 g) cherry tomatoes, sliced in half
8 oz (225 g) mozzarella cheese, cut into bite-size pieces
Salt and pepper

Instructions
1 Cook the fusilli according to the instructions on the package.
   Drain the pasta, then rinse with cold water. Drain it again.
2 Stir in the pesto.
3 Gently fold in the tomatoes and mozzarella, then season with salt and pepper to taste.
4 Chill your salad in the refrigerator until you are ready to serve.

mozzarella

CHEF'S TIP
If your salad seems dry, add a drizzle of olive oil. If it needs more bite, splash in a little lemon juice.

SUMMER PASTA

The key to this recipe is to cook your vegetables until they are just delicious—no more, no less!

You Will Need

14 oz (400 g) fusilli
2 oz (55 g) frozen peas
1 tbsp olive oil
4 oz (115 g) broccoli, chopped into bite-size florets
3 oz (85 g) spinach
½ cup (120 ml) pesto (to make your own, see the recipe on page 23)
Salt and pepper
2 oz (55 g) Parmesan cheese, grated
Basil to garnish

Instructions

1 Cook the fusilli according to the instructions on the package. About four minutes before your pasta will be ready, add the frozen peas to the same pot.
2 While the fusilli and peas are cooking, heat the olive oil in a large frying pan. Add the broccoli and stir-fry for three to four minutes. Now add the spinach, frying it with the broccoli for one minute.
3 When the pasta and peas are cooked, drain them. Add them to the fried broccoli and spinach.
4 Stir in the pesto sauce and season to taste.
5 Transfer to serving dishes, sprinkle with Parmesan cheese, and garnish with basil.

Celebrate summer with this tasty pasta dish!

CHEF'S TIP

For a spicier flavor, add chili flakes to the broccoli as you stir-fry.

CHAPTER 5
AL FORNO

Al forno is Italian for "from the oven." These pasta dishes are baked in the oven until the pasta is soft, the rich sauce is bubbling, and the top is crispy.

From the Oven to the Table

Baked pastas are perfect for serving to guests as they have a more luxurious taste and thicker sauce than pastas served straight from the pan. You can prepare them in advance, filling your kitchen with the smell of delicious food as your guests arrive.

Like most Italian dishes, al forno classics tend to come from particular regions. Lasagna, the worldwide favorite, comes from Naples in southern Italy. Another well-known dish is cannelloni, sometimes called manicotti in the United States. Cannelloni are large tubes of pasta baked with a filling of meat or spinach and ricotta, then covered in tomato or béchamel sauces and baked. Cannelloni probably originated in southern Italy.

Mac and Cheese in the White House

Although mac and cheese has its origins in many cheesy Italian pastas, the dish became most popular in the United States. President Thomas Jefferson, who had eaten macaroni in northern Italy, may have helped the recipe to gain popularity after serving it at a state dinner in the White House in 1802.

Mastering the Basics
Béchamel Sauce

Knowing how to make a béchamel sauce, also called a "white" sauce, is one of the most useful skills any cook can master.

A béchamel is the base for delicious dishes such as lasagna, macaroni or cauliflower and cheese, and fish pies. Here is how to make about 2 cups (480 ml) of sauce:

1 In a saucepan, melt 2 oz (55 g) butter over a low heat.
2 Stir in 2 oz (55 g) all-purpose flour.
3 Slowly, a splash at a time, whisk in 2½ cups (600 ml) milk. Add a bay leaf for flavor if you like.
4 Stir continuously until the sauce has thickened slightly—this means it should drip slowly from a lifted spoon.
5 Season with salt and pepper.

Switch It Up

To make a vegetarian lasagna, follow the recipe on page 30 but use some roasted vegetables instead of the ground beef. Try chopping one eggplant and one red bell pepper, then toss them in 2 tbsp olive oil. Roast them in a large baking pan for about thirty-five minutes at 370°F (190°C). When the vegetables are lightly charred, layer them in the baking pan along with the tomato sauce, béchamel, and lasagna sheets.

LASAGNA

Serving this mouthwatering lasagna will win you some serious respect from friends and family.

You Will Need
1 tbsp olive oil
1 medium onion, peeled and chopped
2 garlic cloves, peeled and crushed
9 oz (255 g) ground beef
3 small carrots, peeled and chopped
15 oz (425 g) can of chopped tomatoes
Salt and pepper
2 cups (480 ml) béchamel sauce (see recipe on page 29)
9 oz (255 g) lasagna sheets
5 oz (140 g) Parmesan cheese, grated

Instructions
1 Preheat the oven to 390°F (200°C).
2 Heat the oil in a large pan, then add the onions and garlic. Fry for four to five minutes until golden, stirring regularly.
3 Add the ground beef and fry for five to six minutes, until brown.
4 Add the tomatoes and carrots to the pan. Season to taste. Cover with a lid and simmer for ten minutes, stirring occasionally.
5 While your meat sauce is cooking, make the béchamel, following the recipe on page 29.
6 To put together your lasagna, spoon one-third of the meat sauce into a large ovenproof dish. Cover with lasagna sheets, then pour over one-third of the béchamel. Repeat this pattern twice more, until you have three layers of meat, lasagna, and béchamel. Sprinkle the Parmesan on top.
7 Bake in the oven for thirty minutes.

The top of your lasagna should be crispy.

CHEF'S TIP

For an even cheesier bake, melt a handful of grated cheese into your béchamel.

MAC AND CHEESE

This cheesy, gooey, crispy baked pasta has to be the perfect comfort food.

This is the perfect meal to share with friends.

You Will Need

8 oz (225 g) macaroni
1 tbsp butter
½ medium onion, peeled and chopped
1 garlic clove, peeled and crushed
1 tbsp all-purpose flour
1½ cups (360 ml) milk
Salt and pepper
7 oz (200 g) cheddar cheese, grated

Instructions

1 Preheat the oven to 350°F (180°C).
2 Cook the macaroni according to the instructions on the package.
3 While the macaroni is cooking, melt the butter in a large saucepan. Add the onion and garlic and cook until golden.
4 Stir in the flour, then slowly stir in the milk. Season with salt and pepper. Stir constantly as the sauce thickens.
5 Slowly add the cheese to the sauce, stirring until it melts.
6 In a large ovenproof dish, mix together the macaroni and cheese sauce.
7 Bake in the oven for thirty minutes.

CHEF'S TIP

To spice up your dish, sprinkle your mac and cheese with 1 tsp (15 ml) of paprika or cayenne pepper before baking.

CHAPTER 6
PASTA SOUPS

Pasta soups are a great way to pack vegetables, proteins, and carbohydrates into a bowl.

Soups Made Simple

To create your own soup recipes, you can use the recipes that follow as a guide, or start with the basic broth shown opposite. When choosing which vegetables to add to your soup, go for your favorites. Root vegetables such as carrots and parsnips work well, but leafy greens like cabbage and spinach add a little texture.

Mix and Match

For protein, you could add legumes, such as cannellini or kidney beans, lentils or chickpeas. If your guests are meat-eaters, throw in bite-sized pieces of cooked ham, chicken, or turkey. Alternatively, use a fish stock as your base and add shrimp or pieces of white fish. To make a really filling soup, add plenty of carbohydrates in the form of your choice of pasta, as well as chunks of potato, and serve with croutons.

Mastering the Basics
Basic Broth

A great soup almost always starts with a delicious broth. Once you have mastered your broth, you can toss in any ingredients you like, from pasta and potatoes to peas and ham. Here is how to make around 4 cups (960 ml) of broth:

1 Chop up one onion, as well as some other vegetables, such as one carrot, one stick of celery, and one leek.

2 In a thick-bottomed saucepan, heat 1 tbsp olive oil, then gently cook the vegetables for ten to fifteen minutes. Keep the lid on, except when stirring.

3 To thicken the stock, coat the vegetables with a tablespoon of all-purpose flour.

4 Pour in 5 cups (1.2 l) chicken or vegetable stock, made from a stock cube or bought at a grocery store. Bring to a boil.

5 Add any other ingredients as well as a bay leaf or a splash of soy sauce for extra flavoring. Continue to simmer until cooked.

Switch It Up

The minestrone on page 36 uses broken spaghetti, and the stracciatella on page 38 uses farfalline, but there are many other mini pastas you could put in your soups. Suitable pastas, known in Italian as *pasta per brodo* ("pastas for soup"), include acini di pepe ("seeds of a pepper"), alfabeto ("alphabet letters"), ditalini ("little thimbles"), orecchiette ("little ears"), and rotelle ("little wheels"). You could also try stuffed pastas, such as tortellini, served in a delicious broth.

MINESTRONE

This hearty soup is traditionally made with whatever pasta and vegetables are in the house.

You Will Need
1 tbsp olive oil
1 medium onion, peeled and chopped
2 medium carrots, peeled and chopped
3 celery sticks, chopped
2 garlic cloves, peeled and sliced
15 oz (425 g) can of chopped tomatoes
5 cups (1.2 l) chicken or vegetable stock
15 oz (425 g) can of cannellini beans
3 oz (85 g) dried spaghetti, broken into short lengths
Salt and pepper

Instructions
1 Heat the oil in a thick-bottomed, large saucepan, then gently cook the onion, carrots, and celery for ten minutes.
2 Add the garlic and fry for one more minute.
3 Add the tomatoes and stock, then simmer for ten minutes.
4 Add the spaghetti and beans, then cook for another ten minutes.
5 Season with salt and pepper and serve hot.

Minestrone is filling, warming, and fun to make.

CHEF'S TIP

For extra flavor, drizzle
your minestrone with a few
teaspoons of pesto sauce
(see page 23).

STRACCIATELLA WITH FARFALLINE

This egg and butterfly pasta soup comes from the region around Rome.

You Will Need
6 cups (1.45 l) chicken or vegetable stock
1 oz (30 g) butter
5 oz (140 g) dried farfalline pasta
4 eggs
2 tbsp fresh parsley, chopped
3 oz (85 g) Parmesan cheese, grated
Salt and pepper

Instructions
1 In a large saucepan, bring the stock to a boil.
2 Add the butter, which will melt.
3 Add the pasta and cook for about eight minutes or according to the instructions on the package.
4 In a mixing bowl, whisk together the eggs, parsley, 2 oz (55 g) of the Parmesan, and a little salt and pepper. Stir this mixture into the pasta and stock.
5 Serve right away, with a sprinkling of Parmesan.

This may be simple, but it is delicious.

To add a spicy, smoky, savory flavor, add a pinch of ground nutmeg to your stracciatella.

CHAPTER 7

PIZZA

A crispy, chewy pizza crust combines perfectly with tomato sauce and soft, stringy mozzarella.

Neapolitan Pizzas

Although people have been eating flatbreads with toppings for thousands of years, modern pizza evolved in Naples, Italy, in the eighteenth century. Pizza was introduced to the United States and around the world by Italian immigrants. Today, you can order pizza to eat in or take out—and, best of all, you can make your own.

Is Pizza Unhealthy?

Mass-produced pizzas probably are unhealthy, as they can be high in salt and saturated fat (in the cheese and any meat toppings). However, homemade pizza, topped with plenty of tomato and other vegetables—with a side of bean salad to provide extra protein—can be an enjoyable part of a balanced diet. To increase your fiber and nutrient intake, use whole wheat rather than refined flour to make your crust.

Mastering the Basics
Pizza Crust

You can buy ready-made pizza dough from the grocery store, but it can be more fun to make your own. Here is how to make two pizza crusts to feed four people:

1. Put 12 oz (340 g) bread flour into a large bowl, then stir in 1 tsp instant yeast and 1 tsp salt.
2. Make a hole, or "well," in the center of the flour, then pour in 1 cup (240 ml) warm water and 1 tbsp olive oil. Mix together until the dough is soft and wet.
3. Put the dough on a flat surface that you have dusted with flour. Knead for five minutes. Put the dough in a lightly greased bowl and cover with plastic wrap. Now leave your dough to rise for a couple of hours, unless you prefer a thin crust pizza.
4. Split the dough into two balls, then use a rolling pin to roll each one into a circle 10 inches (25 cm) across and very thin.
5. Put each crust on a floured baking sheet.

Switch It Up

Once you know how to make pizza crusts and have mastered a basic tomato sauce (see the recipe on page 42), you can add any toppings you like. You could create a classic quattro stagioni ("four seasons") pizza by dividing your crust into four quarters, each with different toppings. For example, the "spring" quarter could be topped with artichokes, the "summer" with mozzarella and tomatoes, the "fall" with mushrooms, and the "winter" with ham and olives.

PIZZA MARGHERITA

This classic pizza was invented in Naples, but today it is a favorite all across the globe.

You Will Need

15 oz (425 g) can of whole tomatoes in juice
1 handful of fresh basil
1 garlic clove, peeled and crushed
Salt and pepper
Two 10-inch (25-cm) pizza crusts (to make your own, see the recipe on page 41)
4 oz (115 g) mozzarella cheese, sliced into rounds
12–16 cherry tomatoes, cut in half
1 tbsp olive oil

Instructions

1 Preheat the oven to 460°F (240°C).
2 To make the sauce, puree the canned tomatoes in a food processor, or press them through a strainer, to make a smooth paste. Using a spoon, mix in the garlic and half of the basil. Season with salt and pepper.
3 Put your pizza crusts on a lightly floured baking sheet or pizza tray. Spread them with the tomato sauce (as much as you need) using the back of a spoon.
4 Dot your pizzas with mozzarella and cherry tomatoes, then drizzle with olive oil.
5 Bake for eight to ten minutes until crisp. Garnish with the remaining basil.

The perfect pizza—and a worldwide favorite.

CHEF'S TIP

For a cheesier topping, sprinkle your pizzas with 2 tbsp of grated Parmesan before baking.

SPINACH CALZONE

These folded pizzas have a delicious filling that will ooze out when you take a bite!

Calzones are easy to eat on the go!

You Will Need

16 oz (450 g) fresh spinach
1 cup (240 ml) ricotta cheese
2 oz (55 g) Parmesan cheese, grated
¼ tsp ground nutmeg
Salt and pepper
All-purpose flour for dusting
Two 10-inch (25-cm) pizza crusts
   (to make your own, see the recipe
   on page 41)

Instructions

1 To make the filling, steam the spinach for about one minute, then drain and squeeze dry.
2 Mix the spinach with the ricotta, Parmesan, and nutmeg, then season with salt and pepper.
3 Place your pizza crusts on a lightly floured baking sheet. Spoon half the filling onto each crust. Fold the crust in half, then pinch and press the edges together to seal it.
4 Cut three slits in the top of each calzone, to let steam escape while cooking.
5 Heat the oven to 450°F (230°C), letting the calzones rest while the oven heats up.
6 Bake the calzones for around twenty to twenty-five minutes, until they look golden brown.

ricotta cheese

CHEF'S TIP

If your calzones leak, roll over the edges before pressing them firmly together.

GLOSSARY

basil An herb with shiny green leaves and a sweet, peppery taste.

béchamel A white sauce made with butter, flour, and milk.

boiling When a liquid is so hot that it releases large bubbles of gas.

browned Cooked until pink meat can no longer be seen.

calories Units used to measure the energy value of food.

carbohydrates Food molecules contained in starchy foods, such as pasta, grains, and potatoes, as well as sugars and fibers. Carbohydrates provide most of your energy.

clove of garlic One of the sections of a bulb of garlic.

crème fraîche A thick cream made from heavy cream with buttermilk, sour cream, or yogurt.

dill An herb with feathery leaves and a slightly bitter taste.

fiber Long molecules that are contained in plants and help with digestion.

frying Cooking in hot oil or another kind of fat.

gluten A mixture of two proteins found in cereal grains such as wheat, barley, rye, and some oats.

intolerance Inability to eat a food without having side effects.

mozzarella A soft white cheese that is traditionally made from buffalo milk.

nutrients Substances found in food that provide essential nourishment for health and growth.

Parmesan A central-Italian hard cheese made from cow's milk.

pesto A sauce made from blended basil, pine nuts, garlic, Parmesan cheese, and olive oil.

protein A substance found in lentils, beans, nuts, seeds, meat, fish, eggs, and dairy products that is essential for growth and health.

refined grains Grains that have had their germ (kernel) and bran (outer layer) removed.

roasted Cooked in the heat of an oven.

saturated fat A type of "unhealthy" fat that is usually found in animal fat products, such as meat and dairy.

simmering Hot enough to bubble gently but not to boil.

stracciatella An Italian soup containing eggs and cheese.

vinaigrette A salad dressing made from oil, vinegar, and seasoning.

whole grain Grain obtained from cereal crops, such as wheat, which have not been processed to break them down.

FURTHER READING

Books:

Bolte, Mari. *Awesome Recipes You Can Make and Share*. North Mankato, MN: Snap Books, 2015.

Editors of Mendocino Press. *The Cookbook for Teens*. Berkeley, CA: Mendocino Press, 2014.

Federman, Carolyn. *New Favorites for New Cooks*. Berkeley, CA: Ten Speed Press, 2018.

Rau, Dana Meachen. *Recipes from Italy*. Chicago, IL: Raintree, 2014.

Websites:

Cooking Tips and Resources
kidshealth.org/en/teens/whats-cooking.html
Discover more cooking tips here.

Kid-Friendly Recipes
www.foodnetwork.com/topics/kid-friendly-recipes
These Food Network pages offer recipes that are easy to cook and healthy.

Recipes and Cooking
kidshealth.org/en/kids/recipes
This is a great list of healthy recipes that are especially made for young cooks.

What Are Carbohydrates?
www.dkfindout.com/us/human-body/keeping-healthy/what-are-carbohydrates
Learn more about carbohydrates, such as those found in pizza and pasta.

Publisher's note to educators and parents: Our editors have carefully reviewed these websites to ensure that they are suitable for students. Many websites change frequently, however, and we cannot guarantee that a site's future contents will continue to meet our high standards of quality and educational value. Be advised that students should be closely supervised whenever they access the Internet.

INDEX